Focus on the Arts and S...
Thematic Units for Early Childhood

7531

by
Diana Courson

illustrated by
Tom Foster

Cover by Tom Foster

Copyright © 1993, Good Apple

ISBN No. 0-86653-750-3

Printing No. 98765432

Good Apple
1204 Buchanan St., Box 299
Carthage, IL 62321-0299

A Paramount Communications Company

Table of Contents

Each unit incorporates art activities as well as art education through the study of a well-known artist.

GA1465

Introduction

This book is one in a set of three books designed specifically for use with preschool through grade two. The series includes *Focus on the Arts and Sciences*, *Focus on America* and *Focus on the World of Work*.

Focus on the Arts and Sciences contains units such as Gravity, Balance and Inertia (physics); Flowers (botany/horticulture); and The Moon and the Stars (astronomy). Each unit provides activities that allow the children to explore, investigate, and construct learning experiences that are meaningful to them. In addition, these science activities have a direct tie to the arts. Well-known artists and works of art are presented with each unit that show a direct tie to the concepts presented in the science activities.

Focus on America provides units such as America's Flag, America's Songs, and America's Legends and Folktales. Each unit offers activities that allow children to learn about the history of Americans and to see a relationship between our country's past and what is happening in their lives today. Teachers are encouraged to adapt the activities to their locale and utilize local resource people; land formations; city, county, and state political agencies; and history.

GA1465

Focus on the World of Work provides units on various occupations with which children should be familiar and provides opportunities for them to explore these jobs using the tools of the trade. A unit on Carpenters shows the tools carpenters need and allows children to use the tools safely in classroom experiences. A unit on Teachers allows children to see the type of work that teachers do both on the job and off. The activities provide a time for children to try the job to see how it feels.

All the thematic units presented in this book are literature-based and culturally sensitive. They integrate various disciplines in an attempt to capitalize on the interests and strengths of individual children as they work in groups to do activities and solve problems. Because the activities are literature-based, they fit well into a whole language classroom. All the units suggest related children's books in order to make the literature connection. These books include those that take a multicultural perspective and offer, when possible, both a current and historical perspective as well.

Thematic units make connections between separate subject areas by becoming the common thread holding an investigation together. The variety of activities in these units helps students connect their learning to real life and thus makes it meaningful. In addition, children are allowed to explore and can construct their own learning activities within those outlined. In this way children can be successful and develop both a positive self-esteem and positive feelings toward learning in general.

The activities in this book are integrated in order to meet the different learning styles and strengths of each child. In its position statement about developmentally appropriate practice for children 5-8 years of age, NAEYC (1987) states

> "The curriculum is integrated so that children's learning in all traditional subject areas occurs primarily through projects and learning centers that teachers plan and that reflect children's interests and suggestions. Teachers guide children's involvement in projects and enrich the learning experience by extending children's ideas, responding to their questions, engaging them in conversation and challenging their thinking. (p. 67)

When all activities and materials suggested in a unit are used, children are active, they explore, and they interact with the materials, adults, and other children. The materials and activities are real, concrete and meaningful to the children. However, in classrooms for preschool through second grade children, additional centers should always be open to allow children to take the knowledge and skills from the thematic units and explore them in the safety of their "home" environment. These centers, like the activities that are presented in the unit, should entice children and motivate them through interaction with a variety of developmentally appropriate materials and equipment. Children may thus choose activities which are of interest to them and become active and interactive learners. These centers might include Art, Blocks, Dramatic Play, Gross Motor, Manipulative, Library, Games. For further ideas on how to set up learning centers for young children, see *Centers for Early Learners Throughout the Year* (GA1334, Good Apple, 1991).

The units in the book contain
- a rationale for selecting the topic which outlines the developmental appropriateness of the topic

- general background information about the topic to be studied

- a listing of three to five books per unit with short summaries (each set of books will attempt to represent at least two cultural groups)

- a variety of activities to include language, math, science, music, movement, self-concept, social/cooperative learning, art, crafts

- one to two reproducible pages per unit which help children record/summarize the information they have learned in order to share it with other children, teachers, and their parents.

Role of the Teacher and Other Adults

The role of the teacher is to find out from the children through interest inventories, parent interviews, child interviews, and observation just what the children are interested in and tie their interests to the curriculum. The teacher spends time preparing the environment for learning, and then talks with the children as they "work" and "play." Adults and older children need to be available to read to children and inquire as children work at their centers and/or on their activities. Children can "read" to other children when the books which have been read to them are left in the library center during free time.

Grouping the Children

For most activities, children can work in small groups, talking with one another, checking one another's progress, guiding one another's learning, and learning from one another. Very seldom do children need to be isolated from others to labor over dittoed work sheets to check to see if they "know" something.

Work Sheets

What work sheets there are in this book are directly tied to each unit and ask the children to record information from the activities in the unit. In this way teachers may see what the children focused on and learned. Parents may discuss the activities with the children when the sheets are taken home. Most of the work sheets are open-ended, allowing children to create their own answers and in some cases construct their own experience.

GA1465

Gravity, Balance and Inertia

Physics

The study of physics may seem to be beyond the abilities of young children. However, some basic components of physics, such as gravity, balance and inertia, are fascinating to children.

Children's Books

Bemelmans, L. (1953). *Madeline's Rescue*. New York: The Viking Press.
When Madeline loses her balance on the bridge, a dog saves the day.

Lefkowitz, R. (1975). *Push! Pull! Stop! Go! A Book About Forces and Motion*. New York: Parents' Magazine Press.
Down-to-earth explanations of beginning physics concepts.

Lovik, C. (1987). *Andy and the Tire*. New York: Scholastic Inc.
Andy learns to balance in order to ride his tire!

Schwartz, J. (1965). *Uphill and Downhill*. New York: McGraw-Hill Book Company.
Excellent book to introduce the unit.

Slobodkina, E. (1947). *Caps for Sale*. New York: Harper.
Eastern European folktale tells the story of a peddler who balances an amazing number of caps on his head.

People to Know

Isaac Newton was a gifted scientist and mathematician. Newton is credited with first identifying the principle of gravity, creating calculus, and many other accomplishments.

Divergent Topics

Sound is an aspect of physics not discussed in this book; it makes an interesting study.

Many circus acts rely on principles of physics. (Your class may be interested in a circus unit.)

1

Background Information

Gravity is the force that holds the universe together. Every object (book, ball, sun, planet, dog) pulls on every other object. Heavy objects have a stonger pull than light objects. This pull is called gravity. The earth's gravity pulls much harder on people, trees, and trucks than it pulls on the earth. Earth's gravity can be overcome only by a stronger force, such as the thrust from a rocket.

In order to *balance*, the pull of gravity must be the same on all sides. The object's *center of gravity* (point where the pull is strongest) must be directly over the point of balance. For example, to stand on one foot, you must shift your body so that your center of gravity is over your foot.

Inertia. About 300 years ago Isaac Newton, a scientist and mathematician, formulated laws of gravity and motion. Newton's first law of motion states that an object that is not moving tends to remain at rest and that a moving object tends to keep moving. This is why it is harder to start and stop a wagon full of blocks than it is to pull it along. More force is required to start and stop movement than to sustain movement. Inertia allows a magician to jerk a tablecloth out from under the dishes set on it. The magician's pull moves the cloth, but the dishes remain at rest.

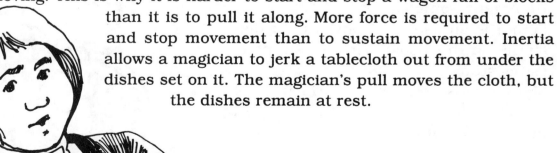

GA1465

Materials needed for investigating, comparing, constrasting, constructing, weighing, dropping, sliding, rolling, balancing:

- blocks of all sizes
- ramps
- small rubber balls
- marbles
- Ping-Pong balls
- 9" x 12" (22.86 x 30.48 cm) (and larger) heavy cardboard for ramps
- beanbags
- small cars and trucks
- small wagon
- toddler-size slide (for objects, not kids!)
- roller coaster (wire and bead maze)
- marble runway construction sets
- toys with gears
- plastic bowling set
- Slinky™ toys
- magnetic marbles
- balance scales and objects to weigh
- games such as tiddlywinks, Don't Spill the Beans, Blockhead

Keep It Up!

Hold out your arms. Try to keep them straight out. Are your arms getting tired? Why? Gravity is pulling them. Your muscles are getting tired of working against gravity.

Rock It and Roll It!

Can you build a seesaw from blocks?

Try to make a ball or car roll uphill.

Can you make a marble roll without touching it?

Drop It!

Can you drop a raw egg without breaking it?

3

GA1465

Musical Statues

Play Musical Statues. Children stop when the music stops and start again with the music. Discuss how hard it is to start or stop suddenly. This activity illustrates inertia. Vary the style of music. What happens?

Physics Games

Play tiddlywinks or Blockhead. Eye-hand coordination is a must for these!

Tell Me All About It!

Each child records (dictates or writes) unit experiences in a lab book. Or the class can make a jumbo lab book on chart paper. Jill wrote the following description of her egg-dropping experience: "First I put the egg in a Ziploc™ bag. Then I lined the sides of a Nike™ box with foam; then I stuffed the bottom with newspaper and then I put the egg in and then I put more newspaper on top and it survived!"

A mini lab book is included with this unit to be reproduced for your class.

Word cards for commonly used words in this unit will help children as they record their activities. Some children who are not ready to write will enjoy playing with the cards.

marble   ball   ramp   hill   gravity   pull

But It Pulled Me Down!

After reading *Caps for Sale* or *Andy and the Tire*, write your own folktales involving gravity or balance.

Roll It and Pat It and Eat It!

Serve a gravity snack: grapes and $1/4$ pieces of graham crackers. Children will need a 9" (22.86 cm) paper plate for this small snack to have room for playing with their food! Roll it, balance it, etc.

GA1465

Exploring Balance

In each space of this paper, trace around one block. You will have three different shapes.

Lay the paper on your desk. Put a block on one shape. Build a stack with only that one block touching the paper.

Try all three shapes as *foundations* for your buildings.

5

Fruit Stack-Ups

Provide cubes of apple, pineapple, pear and cheese. Children stack these up before eating them.

Napkin Magic

Each child will need a lightweight paper napkin and some toasted oat cereal (such as Cheerios™). Children try to pull the napkin out from under their cereal, demonstrating Newton's first law of motion (inertia).

Drip It and Drop It!

Provide several colors of thin paint at the easel. Tell children not to wipe their brushes on the edges of the cups. Press the brush to the paper and let gravity do the painting! Observe the children as they paint. You will see a lot of thinking and planning as they place their brushes on the paper.

Mobiles

Mobiles can be intricate pieces of art. Before the children begin, introduce them to the work of Alexander Calder, a contemporary sculptor who created the first mobiles. Calder's sculptures are made of sheet metal and wire. The mobiles are balanced so carefully that even the slightest breeze will move the pieces. Another artist, Marcel Duchamp, named Calder's moving sculptures "mobiles."

Pictures of Calder's work can be found in art books at the library and in most encyclopedias. Several pictures of these sculptures are essential to help children comprehend the balance involved in designing mobiles.

GA1465

Balance It!

Materials needed: wire, string, yarn, soda straws, feathers, tape, paper punch, wire cutters, ice pick (teacher only!), assorted papers, poster board, many jar lids, bits of Styrofoam™, twigs, pieces of plastic, and more.

Begin the mobile with a strong stick, a sturdy circle of wire, a coat hanger, or other suitable "base." Children tie or tape pieces to wire or string as they put their mobiles together. (Glue is less successful–it is messy and takes too long to dry.)

Provide coat hooks, backs of chairs, or other methods for hanging the mobile as it is created. The child will be able to see and feel the balance problems that arise in the design. Building a mobile on a desk or tabletop does not allow for the experiences with balance. Plastic and metal jar lids are useful as elements in the mobile because they add more weight than paper pieces, emphasizing the need for balance.

Children may discover. . .

that two small pieces will balance one larger piece.

that the placement of the wire or string affects the balance.

that the length of the wire/string doesn't seem to affect the balance.

When the mobile is finished, add a tag with the child's name on one side and the artist's name on the other (in the style of Alexander Calder [1898-1976]).

GA1465

Experimenter's Name _____

Date of Experiment _____

Draw a picture of yourself holding out your arms.

When I held out my arms, they felt
_____
_____
_____
_____
_____
_____

Experimenter's Name _____

Date of Experiment _____

Draw a picture of your experiment with marbles.

Conclusions
_____
_____
_____
_____
_____
_____

Water

Chemistry

Because water is readily available and inexpensive and because it is a familiar material, water is a natural study for young children. As a part of chemistry, children will learn that the same substance can be a gas, a liquid, or a solid and that water is the universal solvent. Water also has a special beauty and power beyond its chemical properties.

Children's Books

Aardema, V. (1981). *Bringing the Rain to Kapiti Plain*. New York: Dial Books for Young Readers, E.P. Dutton, Inc.

An African folktale with cumulative language.

Day, A. (1990). *River Parade*. New York: Scholastic Inc.

Striking illustrations help tell the story of an outing to the river.

Lillegard, D., and Stoker, W. (1987). *I Can Be a Plumber*. Chicago: Children's Press.

Color photographs and simple text detail the plumber's job.

Parramon, J., and Vendrell, C. (1984). *The Four Elements: Water*. New York: Barron's Education Services, Children's Press Choice.

Perfect introductory book for the youngest, easily read by beginners.

Spier, P. (1982). *Rain*. Garden City, NY: Doubleday Company, Inc.

Wordless book with detailed illustrations telling the story of a rain shower from clouds to rainbow.

Wade, H. (1977). *Water*. Milwaukee: Raintree Publishers, Limited.

This book includes basic concepts about water in simple language.

Yashima, T. (1958). *Umbrella*. New York: The Viking Press.

A young girl eagerly awaits the first rainy day to try her new umbrella.

Divergent Topics

Water is an interesting theme for career awareness activities: If you like water, what might you be? (lifeguard, fisher, marine biologist, park ranger, barge pilot, etc.) Water also ties in to geology and meteorology.

9

What Do You Know?

Begin this unit by asking the class, "What do you know about water?" This discussion usually produces varied responses. Record the answers on chart paper. Encourage the children to think of as many answers as they can. Use this information as you plan the unit in order to expand the group's knowledge and experience.

Water Music

Play selections from Handel's *Water Music* for the class. A recording of this work should be easily found at the library or from a music teacher. Handel composed his *Water Music* for King George I. The King's court spent leisure time on barges traveling the Thames River. The barge would anchor at scenic spots, and specially composed music would be played from another barge. This composition was first performed July 17, 1717, on a barge near Chelsea.

After becoming familiar with the music, the group may wish to discuss the name of the work. Is it called *Water Music* because it is about water or because it is written to be performed on water?

The Disappearing Water

Fill a jar with water. Mark the water level with a black permanent marker or a piece of masking tape. Put the jar in an easily observable place but one where it will not be disturbed.

Each day, note the level of the water. Keep a record of evaporation on a chart. When the experiment is concluded, ask the children to change the data collected from a chart form to a graph.

Repeat the experiment with several jars. Place one in the sun; one in a dark, cool place; one near a sink; one outdoors. Are there differences in the rate of evaporation?

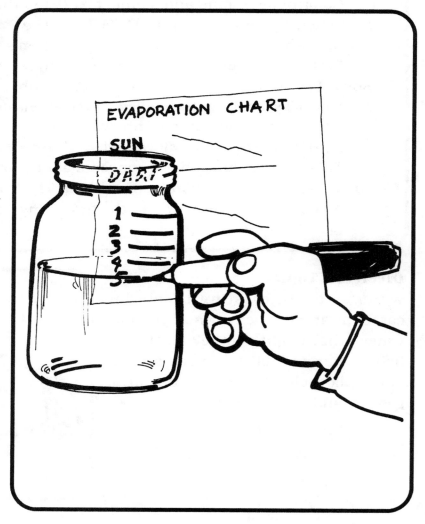

Lucky Ducks

To play Lucky Ducks you will need ten small plastic or rubber ducks or ten small boats. With a permanent marker, write a numeral on the bottom of each toy, 1-10. Float the toys in a large tub of water.

A child picks up one of the ducks/boats, looks at the numeral on the bottom and identifies the numeral. For younger children, this may be the end of their turns. Older children need the challenge of creating a math problem for which the duck's numeral is the answer. For example, the duck has the numeral 7 on it; the child says, "Seven. Two plus five equals seven."

Run and Drip

To observe one of the properties of water (liquids flow), take a stack of 9" x 12" (22.86 x 30.48 cm) sheets of tissue paper outdoors. Hang the tissue paper on a fence or rope at the child's eye level. Provide spray bottles of water for the children to aim at the tissue paper. Demonstrate the spray-and-wait technique. In this way children will take time to watch the water move on the paper before spraying again.

If you place white paper under the tissue paper to catch the drips, you will have another type of water painting as a by-product of the spray activity.

11

GA1465

Not Enough, Too Much?

To illustrate the concept of dissolving, allow the children to mix their own tempera paints. Cover a table with newspaper or a plastic tablecloth.

Provide baby food jars, pitchers of water, small containers of tempera powder, plastic spoons, and paper towels. For children to get the maximum learning from this activity, the teacher must resist the strong urge to explain how much water and how much tempera to use! Let the class discover the proportions needed for the best paint.

Paintbrushes should be nearby so that the children can try out their paints. An easel is great, but $4^{1}/_{2}$" x 6" (11.41 x 15.24 cm) pieces of paper will work just fine for these test swatches.

It may seem that a great deal of paint will be wasted. Some will be. Have storage containers ready for each color that is to be mixed. Provide a few extra containers for those colors that are created as the children work.

Brainwork

For children who need an extra challenge, provide a tub of water, jars, a funnel, a turkey baster, medicine droppers, shells, rocks, and any other interesting items you find. The task is to move the water from one jar to another without dipping or pouring it.

Observe the children as they work. You will see interesting thought processes and teamwork.

GA1465

Wonderful Water

In the space below draw a picture of water. Be sure your picture shows at least three things you have learned about water.

GA1465

Sounds of Water

Write the sound that a river makes. Draw a river.

Write the sound that rain makes. Draw some rain.

Write the sound that snow makes. Draw a snowy picture.

Write the sound that a thunderstorm makes. Draw a storm.

Write the sound the water fountain makes. Draw yourself drinking water.

GA1465

Chemistry

Children encounter the principles of chemistry every day as their snowman melts or the rain puddle dries up. Basic concepts of chemistry lead children to feel more secure in a world that sometimes seems random and disorganized. Children will learn that the physical world is an orderly one and that magic can always be explained.

Children's Books

Gans, R. (1964). *Icebergs*. Englewood Cliffs, NJ: Thomas Y. Crowell Company.

> A preschool/primary level explanation of freezing and melting.

Lefkowitz, R. (1972). *Matter All Around You*. New York: Parents' Magazine Press.

> The sections on matter and gases, liquids, and solids are excellent in helping to explain these concepts.

Lexau, J. (1964). *Benjie*. New York: The Dial Press.

> Young Benjie braves the world to search for his grandma's lost gold earring.

Rumplestiltskin.

> There are many good editions available.

Tobias, T. (1977). *Liquid or Solid? That's a Good Question!* Chicago: Children's Press.

> Simple text, large pictures identify liquids and solids.

People to Know

Rachel Carson was actually trained as a zoologist but is best known for her work in the 1950s and early 1960s which triggered the ecology movement. Her work exposed the dangers of pesticides and other chemicals used in agriculture.

Divergent Topics

Gold is touched on in this unit as one of the elements. Older children will enjoy learning more about gold, from the Gold Rush of 1849 to how jewelry is made. From the study of gases, it is not a big step to learning about the air and stars which are composed mostly of gases.

More Divergent Topics

After learning about gases, children can better understand why they should crawl to escape a smoke-filled house. Combine the chemistry unit with fire safety activities. Literary-minded children may want to explore fairy tales and folklore that use gold or silver as a central plot element.

Background Information

Chemistry is the study of *matter*. Chemists are concerned with the physical properties of matter, including changes that occur when elements are mixed or matter changes from one state to another. Matter is anything that occupies space and has weight. Matter is composed of molecules, atoms, protons, neutrons and electrons.

Matter can exist in three states–*gas*, *liquid*, or *solid*. Temperature and pressure affect matter, causing it to change from one state to another.

Matter is made up of *elements*, which have names, and of combinations of elements. Gold, oxygen, helium, carbon, silver, copper, and fluorine are some elements that we frequently encounter.

It's Element(ary)!

To familiarize children with the names of common elements, collect items made from or representing these elements. Make a word card or a flash card or a sentence strip for each element. Children match the words to the objects.

Examples:
    helium–balloon
    fluorine–toothpaste (fluoride)
    gold–jewelry or candlestick
    silver–flatware or jewelry
    copper–penny
    sodium–salt
    calcium–milk
    iron–nail
    aluminum–can
    carbon–charcoal briquet or coal

Ice in the Desert

Add ice cubes to the sandbox. This is an interesting tactile experience and leads to some logical thinking as children notice the decreasing size of the ice and finally its disappearance.

Back to the Lab

Set up a chemistry lab in your classroom. This might be a table or a tray on the floor. A basic experiment will require water, vinegar, baking soda, empty baby food jars, drinking straw "scoops" and plastic medicine droppers. Do not give instructions other than the basic ground rules—keep everything on the table; do not eat anything; use the tools provided.

Allow the children to discover the excitement of combining baking soda and vinegar.

Afterwards, repeat the experiment as a class demonstration. The children will tell you what to do to produce those wonderful fizzies! As you work through the demonstration, talk about what the bubbles are (carbon dioxide gas); the bubbles are a result of the vinegar and baking soda combining.

At another time include some macaroni in the lab. As the children work they will find that the carbon dioxide bubbles attach to the pasta, raising it to the surface of the jar. As the bubbles burst, the macaroni sinks.

GA1465

Alchemy

Medieval alchemists spent their days trying to turn ordinary elements into gold. This is the basis for the story of Rumplestiltskin. After reading this fairy tale, explain that you know how to change straw into gold.

To accomplish this feat, you will need cheddar cheese, chow mein noodles and a way to melt the cheese (stove, hot plate, electric skillet, etc.). Ask volunteers to chop the cheese into small cubes. Quickly melt the cheese, stirring constantly to avoid burning. Combine the melted cheese and noodles. Drop this concoction by spoonfuls onto wax paper. The cheese cools almost immediately and the snack is ready to eat.

GA1465

Gold Rush

Gold is a precious element because it is difficult to find and it keeps its shine. (Gold doubloons recovered after centuries in the sea remain shiny.) To help children understand how hard it is to find gold, set up an area of the room where they may pan for gold. If you have the space, a small plastic wading pool is perfect. You can also use smaller containers.

Spray paint some gravel gold. Combine the "gold" with other gravel, dirt and sand. Cover the bottom of the container with the gravel mixture. Pour water over the gravel.

Children can use cake pans or sieves from the sandbox to scoop up and shake the gravel, searching for gold. Provide bags for the children to keep their gold in.

Number Whiz

To work with chemistry, you have to be a good mathematician. Math is an important aspect of solving chemistry problems. Also, numbers are used to identify elements and other components of matter. Each element is assigned an atomic number, based on the structure of its atoms. Remind children that if they like chemistry, they need to be good with numbers. Play lots of math games and include lots of numbers in routine activities.

GA1465

Money Laundering

Ask the children to bring in all their old, dirty pennies. After you have a good collection, put out salt and vinegar to clean the pennies. Plastic plates from frozen dinners make good work spaces for this activity.

Each penny needs a pinch of salt and a few drops of vinegar. Children will immediately see that the brillance of the copper is restored by this chemical reaction. If the pennies are examined later, they will be green as the exposed copper oxidizes. This activity is simple but fascinates some children for hours. Not only are they seeing the chemical reaction, but they may also learn the discipline of staying with a tedious project and the value of repeating an experiment.

Growing Crystals

Crystals under a magnifying glass look like tiny cubes. Salt and sugar are crystals. An easy way to watch crystals grow is to add lots of salt to warm water until no more salt will dissolve. Put a craft stick in the cup. Put the cup in a window. Watch each day for crystals to appear on the stick. As the water evaporates, the crystals are left.

GA1465

Melting Art

Wassily Kandinsky (1866-1944) discarded the realistic images of other artists and used colors and shapes to communicate feelings. Kandinsky was a painter, but the children will work with crayons.

A warming tray or electric skillet is required for this project. If a skillet is used, turn it to medium high until it heats up; then turn it to warm. Place folded towels around the edges of the skillet to prevent accidental burns from resting an arm on the edge. As the children work it may be necessary to stop and "reheat" the skillet by turning up the heat, then turning it back down.

When the tray or skillet is ready, place a 4½" x 6" (11.41 x 15.24 cm) piece of white construction paper on it. Children draw with jumbo crayons on the heated paper. Encourage children to draw s-l-o-w-l-y so that the crayon melts as they draw. This is important for obtaining the rich colors and for feeling the chemical change of the crayon from solid to liquid. Basic shapes are used rather than representative drawings.

Completed pictures will be in the style of Wassily Kandinsky.

Note: This will ruin your good crayons. Use old crayons because they will melt! The best crayons are the super jumbo size—more crayon touches the surface of the warm paper, producing more color for less work.

Heat Changes Things

Today we made pictures in the style of Wassily Kandinsky, an artist who used colors and shapes. Kandinsky was a painter, but we used crayons and paper. List the things you did to make your picture.

First, I _____

_____

Next, I _____

_____

This is what happened: _____

_____

While I was drawing, it felt _____

_____

If I did this again, I would _____

_____

Wind
Meteorology

Children are more aware of weather than are many adults. Good weather brings hours of outdoor playtime; bad weather means trying to avoid boredom indoors. Because wind can sometimes be frightening, this unit may be valuable in helping children understand wind and overcome some of their fear.

Children's Books

Hatch, S. (1973). *Wind Is to Feel*. New York: Coward, McCann and Geoghegan, Inc.

    Descriptive language and illustrations.

Hutchins, P. (1974). *The Wind Blew*. New York: Macmillan Publishing Company.

    In a few words the author tells the story of a windy day.

Martin, C. (1987). *I Can Be a Weather Forecaster*. Chicago: Children's Press.

    Full-color photographs illustrate the narrative of a weather forecaster's career.

McCloskey, R. (1957). *Time of Wonder*. New York: The Viking Press.

    The classic story of late summer in New England and gale force winds.

McKissack, P. (1988). *Mirandy and Brother Wind*. New York: Alfred A. Knopf.

    In this African American story, a young girl tries to capture the wind.

Nodset, J. (1963). *Who Took the Farmer's Hat?* New York: Scholastic Inc.

    The wind blows the farmer's hat away, but no one sees it as a hat!

Divergent Topics

Other aspects of weather might be explored in conjunction with this unit. Wind has an important impact on flight; students may be interested in airplanes, hot air balloons, kites or other forms of flight. Sailing is another form of travel influenced by wind, and some children will be fascinated by sailboats.

GA1465

Writing the Wind

Familiar children's poems have been written about wind. Robert Louis Stevenson and Christina Rosetti are two authors whose work you will recognize. ("I saw you toss the kites on high. . . ." and "Who has seen the wind?")

After sharing some poetry with your class, invite children to write their own poems. A simple pattern might be to make the sound of the wind, describe what the wind does and then tell what happens because of the wind.

Example: Whoosh! Whoosh!
             My hair in my face!
             Turn around, hair behind!

Example: No sound at all
             Leaves not moving
             Put away the kite.

Compile the class poems to share with parents and school administrators.

The Farmer's Hat

Read *Who Took the Farmer's Hat?* Has the wind ever blown something of yours? Did you get it back? Use the pattern to make hat shapes from brown construction paper, one for each child. Encourage children to turn the hat shapes around, considering what they might be if they are not hats. When a child has an idea, he or she glues the hat to a piece of drawing paper, adding the details of the picture with crayons. The child then writes (or dictates) a sentence such as "It's a hat, but it might be a rocking chair."

GA1465

The Cakewalk

Read *Mirandy and Brother Wind* with your class. Provide time and space for children to practice the movements they imagine from the story. Remind them to arch their backs, point their toes, and hold their heads high.

Mark off a large square in the classroom or outdoors for the cakewalk. To add an extra challenge, tape large numeral cards inside the square. Each child uses his or her best junior cakewalk form to move to the correct numeral after you give a problem. For example, with younger children who recognize numerals, you call out, "Three!" The child moves to the numeral 3. For older children, state a math fact or problem: "2 + 6 = ?" The child moves to the numeral 8. Provide paper cupcakes (or real cupcakes) for everyone when the game is over.

Catch the Wind

Mirandy worked hard to catch the wind so that he would have to do her bidding. Your more inventive children will be intrigued by the problem of trying to catch the wind. Ask them to draw or write their solutions and post these in the classroom.

Initiate a small group or whole class discussion of what would be asked of Brother Wind if we succeeded in catching him. You may want to record these responses to add to the "Catching the Wind" bulletin board.

GA1465

Wind Wheel

Cut out the large square on this page. Color it on both sides. Then cut the dotted lines toward the center. Pull the corners to the center. Attach to the eraser of a pencil with a straight pin. Bend the pin up to hold the wind wheel in place. Experiment with the wheel on a windy day or when creating wind indoors.

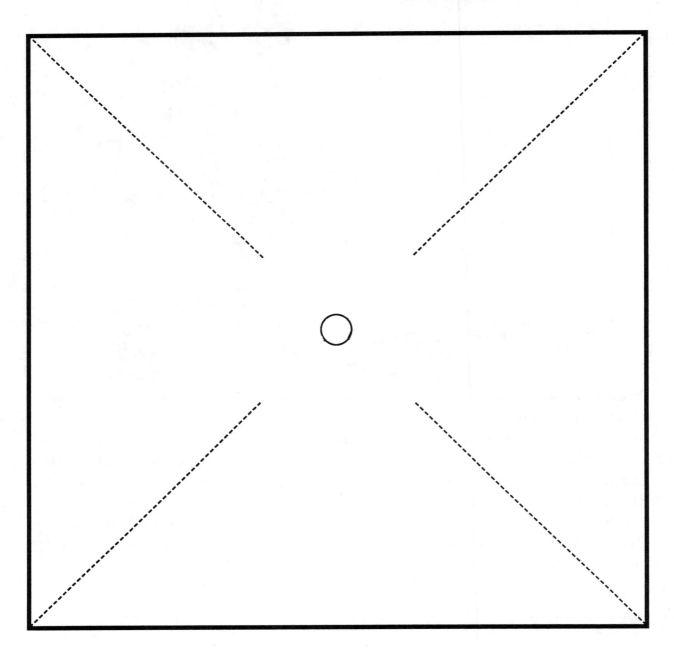

GA1465

Wind Races

The wind helps us get our work done. To demonstrate this, have children paint with water on the chalkboard or on the sidewalk outdoors. Allow part of the wet areas to dry in the air; use paper fans or other wind makers to dry some areas. Time the drying. Wind speeds evaporation.

Make sailboats from wood, Styrofoam™, or bath soap. Add paper, cardboard, plastic, or fabric sails. Sail the finished boats in a large tub. Use paper fans or allow children to blow into the sails to move the boats.

Did You Water the Wind?

The idea of wind farms sounds strange to children. These are "farms" of wind-mills that generate electricity. Guide the class on a search for information about wind farms.

It's Gonna Blow!

Storms are sometimes frightening. *Time of Wonder* shows a family singing through a windstorm. Wind is moving air; sometimes the air moves faster than a car! Talk with the children in a reassuring way about what to do in case of a windstorm in your area. Thanks to modern meteorology, we usually know in advance that a storm is coming and can take shelter.

GA1465

Blow, Wind, Blow!

Show the class examples of the work of Jackson Pollock. This artist tried to get away from images in art and replace these with sensations. Pollock's style and technique have been called action painting. Rather than applying paint with a brush, Pollock might stand in the middle of a huge canvas and sling paint from a bucket.

To simulate Pollock's work, children can use wind to spread the paint. Each child will need a plastic soda straw and access to containers of tempera. (Experiment with the paint until it is just the right consistency to spread.) To make a "wind painting," the child drops some paint onto the paper with the straw, then blows through the straw to spread the paint. The end of the straw should be close to, but not touching, the paint when blowing.

Vary the results by using different color combinations and different papers. In this way the painting can also be tied to a special season or holiday.

Mount the finished paintings on poster board or construction paper. Write "In the Style of Jackson Pollock (1912-1956)" on each painting.

GA1465

Watching the Wind

We have been learning about wind. We have learned that wind is moving air. Sometimes it moves slowly and sometimes very fast. Watch the weather report on television, or read about it in the newspaper. Record information about the wind for four days. Were there any changes in the wind?

Day One

Wind speed: _____

Wind blows from: _____

Other information: _____

Day Two

Wind speed: _____

Wind blows from: _____

Other information: _____

Day Three

Wind speed: _____

Wind blows from: _____

Other information: _____

Day Four

Wind speed: _____

Wind blows from: _____

Other information: _____

GA1465

Rocks, Sand and Mud
Geology

What could be closer to a child's heart than dirt! This unit will help children look carefully at geology, learning about different types of rocks, how sand is made, and why mud may be good.

Children's Books

Brown, M. (1947). *Stone Soup*. New York: Charles Scribner's Sons.
   The classic folktale of soup made from a stone.

Cohlene, T. (1990). *Ka-ha-si and the Loon: An Eskimo Legend*. Vero Beach, FL: The Rourke Corporation, Inc.
   This legend explains earthquakes.

Jennings, T. (1982). *Rocks and Soil*. Chicago: Children's Press.
   Excellent photographs and drawings illustrate the concepts of minerals, volcanoes, fossils, glaciers, and more.

Sipiera, P. (1986). *I Can Be a Geologist*. Chicago: Children's Press.
   The work of a geologist is told in simple text and clear illustrations.

Steig, W. (1969). *Sylvester and the Magic Pebble*. New York: Windmill Books.
   This Caldecott award winner tells the story of Sylvester Duncan who finds a magic pebble and becomes a rock himself.

Wood, J. (1991). *Caves: An Underground Wonderland*. Milwaukee: Gareth Stevens Children's Books.

Divergent Topics

Geology is a beginning point for many investigations. Try a whole unit on caves, volcanoes, earthquakes, or jewels. Children may want to find out more about desert life or shore life, or they may be eager to dig into fossils and paleontology.

GA1465

Singing Rocks

Teach the class this simple song to the tune of "The Pawpaw Patch."

Digging in my sandbox, find a pebble,
Digging in my sandbox, find a pebble,
Digging in my sandbox, find a pebble,
Pick it up and keep it.

Verse 2: Walking on the beach, find a seashell.
Verse 3: Rock in my shoe, take it off and shake it.
Verse 4: Rocks in a cave, stand up, hang down.
Verse 5: Shiny rocks, shiny rocks, might be diamonds!
Verse 6: Big rocks, little rocks, all around us.

Wet and Dry

Sand is found in arid and wet areas. Children can choose to make a beach or a desert picture. Spread watery glue on construction paper; sprinkle sand over the glue. Add beach or desert things with markers or by cutting shapes from construction paper and gluing to the sand.

Magic Rocks

After reading *Sylvester and the Magic Pebble*, children describe what they would do if they had a magic pebble. Write these short stories at the bottom of 9" x 12" (22.86 x 30.48 cm) drawing paper; the children add illustrations. The class set of magic pebble stories makes a great book.

Rock and Roll

Involve the class in collecting rocks. Small groups of children can then explore the rock collection. Here are some things they may do:

Weigh the rocks.

Measure the circumference.

Sort the rocks.

Measure the length of rocks.

Try to roll the rocks.

Try to draw with the rocks.

Draw on the rocks.

Build with the rocks.

Glorious Mud

In the classroom or outdoors, provide a tub of sand, a tub of mud, and a tub of dirt. Allow time for all children to get their hands into each tub. Then add small shovels, butter tubs, plastic worms, and other tools that will expand the children's exploration.

As a follow-up activity, use the evaluation form on the next page.

Paper Spelunker

To make paper caves, each child will need a brown lunch bag, 6" x 4½" (15.24 x 11.41 cm) poster board, Play-Doh™, and markers or crayons. Cut about 3"

(7.62 cm) off the top of the lunch bag. Glue the bag to the poster board to make the cave. Add grass, rocks and trees with markers and construction paper. Use the Play-Doh™ to form stalactites and stalagmites; attach these inside the cave. Some kids will want to add bats, cave fish and other creatures.

GA1465

Messy Day

We played in sand, mud and dirt today. This is what I think about it.

Sandbox

The sand felt _____ and _____.

In the sand I could _____

_____.

Mud Box

The mud felt _____ and _____.

In the mud I could _____

_____.

Dirt Box

The dirt felt _____ and _____.

In the dirt I could _____

_____.

The best part was _____.

I would like to do this again _____ Yes _____ No

I didn't like it when_____

_____.

GA1465

Just Add Water!

Add water to sand, dirt and rocks. What happens?

Sand

A little water:

A lot of water:

Dirt

A little water:

A lot of water:

Rocks

A little water:

A lot of water:

I learned _____

The Moon and the Stars

Astronomy

Many principles and concepts of astronomy are difficult for children to comprehend because they are not readily visible. However, children are naturally curious about the moon and stars; they can begin to learn about these aspects of the universe.

Children's Books

Carle, E. (1977). *Papa, Please Get the Moon for Me.* New York: Scholastic Inc.

  The author cleverly demonstrates the phases of the moon.

Cohlene, T. (1990). *Quillworker: A Cheyenne Legend.* Vero Beach, FL: The Rourke Corporation, Inc.

  A Native American legend explains how the constellations were made.

Fowler, A. (1991). *The Sun Is Always Shining Somewhere.* Chicago: Children's Press.

  Beautiful photographs illustrate this beginning reader that explains the sun's characteristics.

Wandelmaier, R. (1985). *Now I Know: Stars.* Mahwah, NJ: Troll Associates.

  Basic information about stars with lovely watercolor illustrations.

People to Know

Maria Mitchell was the first woman astronomer in the United States. She identified a comet and was awarded a medal for her work.

Divergent Topics

It is difficult to talk about astronomy without including activities on space travel. NASA has excellent materials available (free) for teachers. Write to Johnson Space Center in Houston. Be sure to state the grade you teach and the number of students.

GA1465

Does the Moon Grow?

Young children may not easily understand that the moon does not really change its size during the month, that it only appears different to us. Try reading *Papa, Please Get the Moon for Me*. Even very young children know that the little girl's papa could not really get a ladder, climb up and get the moon. This story gives a good starting point for discussing the moon. Ask the class to observe the moon several times so that they see the differences through the month. From the group's observation or from an almanac or newspaper, record the moon's phase on the classroom calendar.

Starry Night

Vincent Van Gogh produced striking paintings of the night sky. One of his most famous is the *Starry Night* painting. Give children many opportunities to examine Van Gogh's work.

Provide art supplies for children to use in creating a night sky picture. Include assorted papers, paints, markers, glue, metallic gift wrap, scraps from mylar balloons, etc.

Counting the Stars

New stars are discovered or named frequently. It seems an impossible task to count the stars. Children can count the "stars" in this game, however. Cut stars from 4" x 6" (10.16 x 15.24 cm) index cards, a different number of stars on each card. (If stars are too difficult to cut, simply cut small circles.)

Put one card at a time on the overhead projector. Children count the stars they see. When more challenge is needed, remove the cards quickly so that children must count as fast as possible.

Constellation Creations

After learning about some of the constellations in the sky, children may want to reproduce some constellations or create their own. For this activity you will need blue or black construction paper (9" x 12" [22.86 x 30.48 cm]), a piece of foam at least $1/2$" (1.25 cm) thick and as large as the paper, and a push-pin. Lay the paper on the foam; push the pin through the paper to create a star. When the constellation is completed, hang the paper in the window to see the night sky.

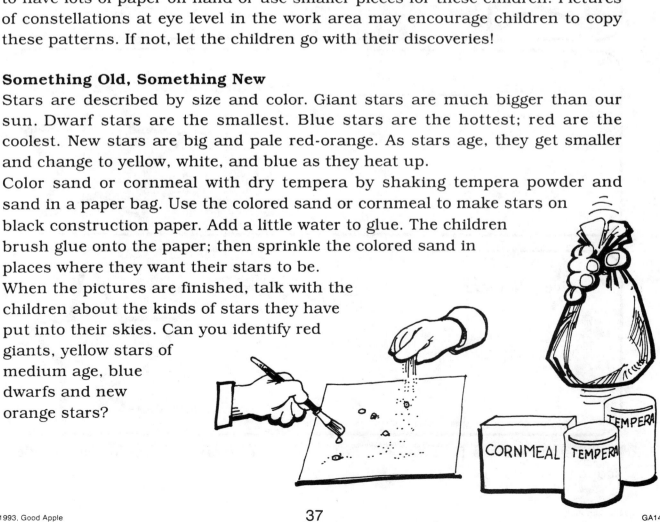

Some children will become so involved with the process that they will end up with a pincushion effect. Plan to have lots of paper on hand or use smaller pieces for these children. Pictures of constellations at eye level in the work area may encourage children to copy these patterns. If not, let the children go with their discoveries!

Something Old, Something New

Stars are described by size and color. Giant stars are much bigger than our sun. Dwarf stars are the smallest. Blue stars are the hottest; red are the coolest. New stars are big and pale red-orange. As stars age, they get smaller and change to yellow, white, and blue as they heat up.

Color sand or cornmeal with dry tempera by shaking tempera powder and sand in a paper bag. Use the colored sand or cornmeal to make stars on black construction paper. Add a little water to glue. The children brush glue onto the paper; then sprinkle the colored sand in places where they want their stars to be.

When the pictures are finished, talk with the children about the kinds of stars they have put into their skies. Can you identify red giants, yellow stars of medium age, blue dwarfs and new orange stars?

Star Colors

Color each star on this page. Write the color word in the space.

A new star is _____.

A very old star is a _____ _____.

The sun is _____. It is a medium star.

A very hot star is _____.

Many stars are too far away for us to see their colors. We would need a telescope to see them.

38

I Might Be an Astronomer

We know a lot about the stars and the moon, but there is a lot to learn. Would you like to be an astronomer and study the stars? What would you like to find out?

I would/would not like to be an astronomer because _____

_____.

If I could be an astronomer, I would like to find out _____

_____.

Draw a picture of some of the tools you would need to be an astronomer.

GA1465

Light

Optics

The study of light is an area of physics that is important to children. Some may be afraid of the dark, and all children value sunlight because they can then play outdoors.

Children's Books

Fowler, A. (1991). *The Sun Is Always Shining Somewhere*. Chicago: Children's Press.

    Large, clear photographs illustrate the sun's importance to us and why we can't see the sun at night.

Greenfield, E. (1976). *First Pink Light*. New York: Thomas Y. Crowell Company.

    A young child is waiting for Daddy to come home. He finally arrives with the first pink light of day.

Jennings, T. (1982). *Light and Color*. Chicago: Children's Press.

    Comprehensive discussion of the subject for primary children with many illustrations. Includes "Things to Do" and "Experiments to Try."

Orii, E., and Orii, M. (1989). *Simple Science Experiments with Light*. Milwaukee: Gareth Stevens Children's Books.

    Large pictures illustrate step-by-step experiments for the very youngest as well as for older children.

Divergent Topics

This unit is an excellent companion to units on astronomy or shadows. Color and camouflage are interesting to children. A unit on rainbows is fun and can become an end-of-the year celebration. After learning about light, some children may want to continue exploring how we see.

GA1465

Traveling Light

Light travels in a straight line. Use a flashlight, study lamp, or slide projector to show children that the light does not curve. Challenge children to devise ways to make light go around corners. (Try using a mirror.)

Bend It; Color It

White light (sunlight) is composed of the seven colors of the spectrum: red, orange, yellow, green, blue, indigo, violet. When the light travels in a straight line, we see white light: when the light is bent, we may see different colors. This bending of light is called *refraction*.

Raindrops refract light when they produce a rainbow. Looking through the spray of a garden hose can produce the same effect. A prism in the classroom will help children see the colors of the spectrum. Place the prism near a window that gets a lot of sun. Children experiment with moving the prism to produce rainbows. (Be prepared for the rest of the class to get very excited when rainbows begin flying around the room!)

Shining Through!

Light shines straight through clear things like water, glass, and plastic wrap. These things are *transparent*. Some things allow light to shine through, but it does not come straight through; these materials are *translucent*. Fabric, paper, and fiberglass awnings are translucent.

In a dark corner of the room put out a tray of transparent and translucent items, along with a flashlight. Children experiment with the objects on the tray

and sort them according to their action on the beam of light.

Expand the activity by inviting children to test other objects in the room and in the building to determine whether they are transparent, translucent, or *opaque* (no light comes through).

41

Flashlight Days

Designate a day or days as Flashlight Day(s). Ask each child to bring a flashlight (with fresh batteries!) to use in the day's activities. Be sure each flashlight has the child's name on it. As the children arrive, have them put their flashlights in their cubbies or put all the flashlights in a large basket.

Flashlight Tag

Darken the classroom as much as possible. Allow the children to play with the flashlights on the ceiling for a few minutes. Remind children that a flashlight is used to illuminate something, not to shine in another person's face or eyes. Notice how straight the rays of light are from the flashlights to the ceiling. To play flashlight tag, children try to "catch" another light while avoiding being caught. (This is great for visual figure-ground exercise! Children have to follow their own light among many.)

Flashlight Find It

Before the game, mount 6" (15.24 cm) shapes of different colors on the ceiling or high up on the walls. Darken the room. When you call out a color and/or shape, the children shine their lights on that color/shape. For example, "Find the large red circle." The children shine their flashlights on a large red circle. Letters, numerals, or other symbols might be used for older children.

Flashlight Snack

Before class prepare red, yellow, green, and orange gelatin. You might have a class committee make the gelatin the day before. Put a spoonful of each color in a clear plastic cup. Each child will have a cup of colors; shine the flashlight through the colors onto the desks, ceilings, walls. Try to shine through only one color or several colors at once. Finally, eat it!

Flashlight Walk

Prepare a darkened route through the building. Close doors on a hallway; cover windows. Guide the children with their flashlights; remember to use the flashlight to light the floor as you walk. Stop along the way to make light circles on the wall or to find the fire extinguisher, etc.

GA1465

Mirror, Mirror

All objects *reflect* some light (this is how we see things); smooth, shiny things stop the light and bounce it back. Provide different kinds of mirrors for the children to explore. Include some items that we usually don't think of as mirrors: pots, mylar, aluminum foil, hubcaps. Make a class chart of the children's discoveries about mirrors.

Mirrors and Monet

Claude Monet (1840-1926) explored the changes that light and atmosphere bring about in the look of an object. Some of his later paintings blotted out the actual shapes of objects and showed blobs, trails, flourishes, and tangles of color. Many of Monet's paintings are of the same subjects at different times of day or different times of the year. A very popular impressionist, Monet is an artist whose work is readily available at the public library and on calendars.

Help the class compare Monet's paintings of Parliament buildings. Notice the differences that the light makes in how we see things.

To create a painting in the style of Monet, you will need a set of watercolor paints and a brush, a small container of water, a small sponge, a mirror 9" x 12" (22.86 x 30.48 cm) or smaller, and white construction paper the same size as the mirror. The child paints on the mirror with the watercolors. Since Monet often used the colors purple, blue, green, and yellow, you might cover the other colors in the box with masking tape. Encourage children to swirl the paint on the mirror. When the mirror is covered with paint, lay the white paper over the mirror, rub the paper and lift it to see the print. These prints are very striking when mounted or matted with purple construction paper.

GA1465

We Use Light

Here are some of the things we use that must have light. Write a few words about each one that you try this week.

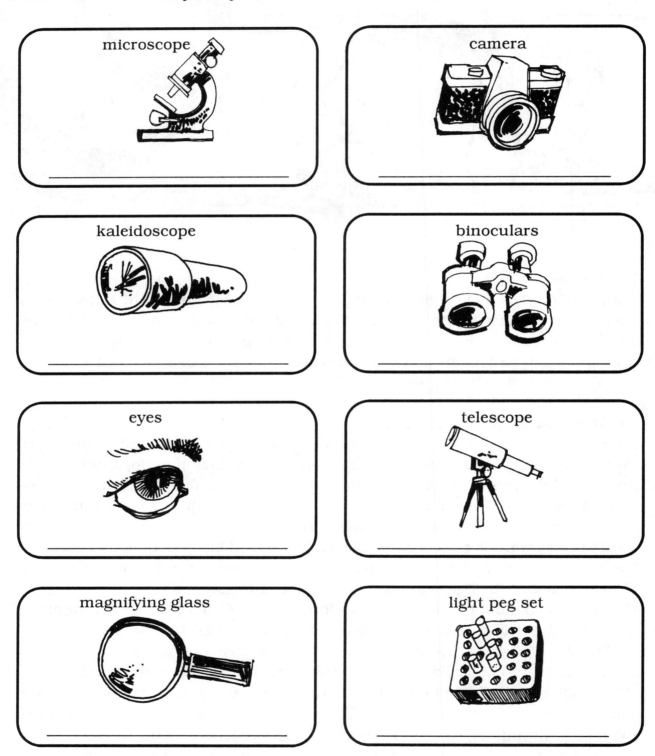

microscope

camera

kaleidoscope

binoculars

eyes

telescope

magnifying glass

light peg set

44

First Light, Last Light

Watch the sunset for a week. Record the colors of light that you see each day. Use crayons to show the colors or name the colors.

1	2	3	4

5	6	7

Try to see a sunrise one day. Record the colors of light that you see. Are these colors the same as or different from the sunsets?

Shadows

Optics

Shadows are fun, but some shadows can be frightening to children. Learning about shadows helps children understand the dark shapes they see in the night.

Children's Books

Asch, F. (1985). *Bear Shadow*. New York: Scholastic Inc.
   A little bear tries everything to make his shadow behave.

Brown, M. (1982). *Shadow*. New York: Macmillan Publishing Company.
   Retelling of this African tale with Marcia Brown's award-winning illustrations.

Bulla, C. (1962). *What Makes a Shadow?* Englewood Cliffs, NJ: Thomas Y. Crowell Company.
   This book of facts about shadows is written especially for young children.

Charlip, R. (1966). *Mother, Mother, I Feel Sick; Send for the Doctor Quick, Quick, Quick!* New York: Parents' Magazine Press.
   Hilarious shadow play of a boy who failed to eat right.

Goor, R., and Goor, N. (1981). *Shadows: Here, There, and Everywhere*. New York: McGraw-Hill Book Company.
   Stunning black-and-white photographs illustrate this examination of shadows.

Simon, S. (1970). *Let's-Try-It-Out: Light and Dark*. New York: McGraw-Hill Book Company.
   This book combines an explanation of shadows and light with simple experiments.

Yolen, J. (1987). *Owl Moon*. New York: Philomel Books.
   Caldecott award-winner's beautiful illustrations of a shadowy winter night.

Divergent Topics

Children who are intrigued by the changes in shadows caused by the earth's rotation may enjoy investigating methods of telling time. The art of cutting silhouettes is a natural topic related to shadows. Use the contrast of light and shadow as a lead-in to a discussion of opposites.

Blob Shadows

Fold a piece of white construction paper in half. Unfold it. Drip some black paint in the center. Fold the paper again and rub it, pushing the paint away from the fold. Open the paper to see the shadow. Give the shadow a name.

Does Your Shadow Measure Up?

Go outdoors and measure shadows in the school yard. Measure the shadow of the same object at different times during the day. Guide children as they explain the reason for the changes in the shadows.

Ask children to find ways to make shadows larger and smaller. (As an object moves closer to or away from the light source, it becomes larger or smaller.)

Whole Child Shadows

To make whole child shadows, you will need a strong light source, such as a slide or filmstrip projector. Shine the light on a large blank wall or hang a sheet on the wall for a screen. Give children time to play with shadows their bodies can make. Then offer a few props such as a broom, a scarf, or a chair. Encourage children to create shadow scenes using props. Remember that a shadow can give the illusion of one object but actually be another object.

GA1465

Shadow Matchups

Trace the shapes of objects on a piece of poster board. Color the shapes black. The child matches the real object to its shadow. Vary the difficulty of the game by turning the objects in unusual positions to trace the shadows. Hint: Cookie cutters are easy to trace and easy to match.

Shadows Overhead

Set up an overhead projector in your classroom during this unit. Provide objects for the children to manipulate on the projector which will cast interesting shadows. Look for smooth plastic and rubber objects which will not scratch the glass surface of the projector. A comb, a bristle block and a toothbrush are often popular items.

Extend this activity by providing easel paper for children to draw the projected shadows. These shadows can then be painted in the art center, cut out and added to a shadow bulletin board.

Shadow Sandwich

Make simple shadow sandwiches with one slice of white bread, one slice of whole wheat or dark rye bread and your favorite filling. A small group of "chefs" might make enough for the whole class to share.

Night Shadows

Use a globe and a flashlight to demonstrate that night is a shadow. The flashlight is the sun; as the earth rotates, we are on the opposite side in the earth's shadow. Use a piece of poster board to show how clouds cast shadows on the earth. On cloudy days we are in the clouds' shadow.

Funny Shadows, Mysterious Shadows

Read *Mother, Mother, I Feel Sick; Send for the Doctor Quick, Quick, Quick!* by Remy Charlip. Encourage the children to create their own shadow story by making shadow puppets. Draw and cut out the characters from poster board. Attach a flexible soda straw to the back of each puppet with tape.

To present the shadow story, children will need a strong light source, a screen, and an audience. The puppets for this play are between the light and the screen. Children will need to practice to find just the right distance between the light and screen for the best image. If longer puppet sticks are needed, squeeze the end of a plastic straw and insert in the open end of the puppet straw.

To maximize cooperative learning experiences, you may want to assign the children to groups. Some of the groups will want to perform their puppet shows for other groups or classes. Remind the audiences to be generous with their applause because the puppeteers have worked hard on this project.

Light Makes a Shadow

Shadows change if the light changes. Draw the shadows for the objects below. Be sure to draw the shadow away from the light.

Which Shadow Fits?

Cut out the shadow cards at the bottom of the page. Match them to the pictures.

GA1465

Architecture

Basic concepts of architecture for young children consider the work of the architect, building materials and features of a building.

- An architect plans what a building will look like and where the rooms will be.
- An architect considers the environment and the climate in selecting bulding materials.
- There are many different doors, windows and roofs.
- Buildings must be strong and should be pleasant to look at.

Children's Books
Barton, B. (1981). *Building a House*. New York: Greenwillow Books.
   The large clear illustrations and simple text are great for very young children and for beginning readers.
Hoberman, M. (1978). *A House Is a House for Me*. New York: The Viking Press.
   This book begins by considering different types of shelter, but the fanciful illustrations and lilting language soon take a creative turn.
Macaulay, D. (1978). *Castle*. New York: Houghton.
   Drawings illustrate the building of a castle. By the same author as *Cathedral*.
The Three Little Pigs vividly illustrates the necessity of choosing appropriate materials for one's house.

People to Know
Examples of the work of renowned architects will be of interest during this unit. Thomas Jefferson, Christopher Wren and Frank Lloyd Wright are included in encyclopedias and other resources. Studying these architects will help students understand the interrelationships of environment, need and beauty.

Divergent Topics
Consider extending the unit to learn about castles, engineering, climate or topography.

By the Rules

Children always enjoy ruler drawings! Provide a variety of rulers, plain paper (4½" x 6" [11.41 x 15.24 cm] is a good size), and lots of pencils. Colored pencils add an important feeling to the activity. Remind children to measure and plan their designs. Extend the activity by offering protractors and other tools for drawing angles, curves, squares, and for lettering.

What Are You Looking At?

Ask children to describe what they see when they look out the classroom window. What about a window at your house? Recall the different sizes and shapes of windows that the class has seen. Windows let in light and allow us to look out. Windows also contribute to the beauty of a building. Give the children large paper windows; they draw what they might see when they look out that window. A short neighborhood walk will help children think of different types of windows and will give them ideas for what they might see from each window.

Blocks of Blocks

Gather as many blocks as you can: wooden unit blocks, small table blocks, inch cubes, cardboard blocks. Add to these blocks some homemade blocks: milk cartons stuffed with newspaper and sealed with tape and boxes of all sizes. Finally, provide flat sheets of cardboard.

Tell the children that they are to become architects. They will design and build houses, but they must use only the building materials that are available in the area. They may work in pairs or small groups, or they may work alone. First they will plan their structures, drawing their designs on paper. Then they will build their designs with the blocks in the room.

As the class works, observe the ways in which children solve problems of balance and design and how they work together sharing ideas. When the structures are completed, take photographs of the children with their buildings. Mount the designs near the buildings. The class may wish to invite other classes or parents to tour their city.

53

Just a Facade

Through pictures or a field trip, explore the fronts of buildings. Note that older buildings often have elaborately detailed facades, while newer buildings may 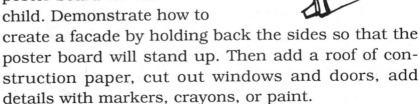 have more streamlined facades.

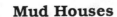

Cut one piece of 12" x 14" (30.48 x 35.56 cm) poster board for each child. Demonstrate how to create a facade by holding back the sides so that the poster board will stand up. Then add a roof of construction paper, cut out windows and doors, add details with markers, crayons, or paint.

Mud Houses

Children need the opportunity to work with real clay rather than Play-doh™. Red or gray clay is available at craft stores and from school supply dealers. Be sure that the clay can be air dried or dried in your oven. You will need about ½ pound (.225 kg) of clay for each child.

A piece of wax paper defines the child's work space at a desk or table. Tools needed include 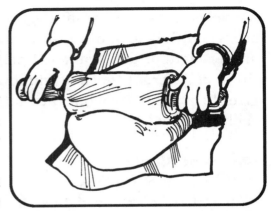 craft sticks, plastic knives, and toothpicks. A small bowl of water needs to be within reach of each child. Allow plenty of time for this project. The children will need some time to experiment with the clay before they actually start building.

The easiest building technique is the flat wall structure. Roll out the clay. Cut out walls with a plastic knife. Join the walls by smoothing water on the corners with fingertips. Children will devise other methods; encourage each child's ideas.

Doors, windows, and other details are added with a knife or toothpick. These may be put in before the walls are put together. Plan a place for the structures to dry. If each child's wax paper is slipped onto a piece of cardboard, the clay house can be easily carried to a shelf or table. The clay usually dries in 24 to 28 hours, depending on the thickness of the structure. Tempera and acrylic paints can be used to finish the project.

GA1465

Don't Eat the House!

Edible houses are fun to build and fun to destroy. You will need lots of graham crackers, plastic knives, and peanut butter. Children use peanut butter as mortar to join the graham cracker "bricks." These may be flat houses, cube houses or stacked houses. Each child will need a paper plate to use as a work space. The houses may be eaten immediately or saved until all are completed and then devoured together!

Our House

Divide the class into small groups. Provide an appliance box for each group. Each group will plan and create a building using the appliance box. The focus on this activity is cooperation; adults will intervene as little as possible. If the weather is suitable, this is a great outdoor event.

The class will need assorted papers, paints, markers, and crayons. Fabric scraps and yarn add another option for decoration. This project is a good place to use the wallpaper samples your school has collected. Adults will need to be available to cut out windows and doors for the children.

Family Field Trip: Architecture

Take a walk or a drive with your child. Look for roofs, windows, doors, and different types of building materials. Record your observations and return this page to school on _____. Have fun!

We saw roofs that looked like this.

We saw windows that looked like this.

We saw doors that looked like this.

We saw buildings made out of these things._____

_____

_____

_____

Name_____

A House Is a House . . .

Read the book *A House Is a House for Me* by Mary Ann Hoberman. Write your own story using Ms. Hoberman's language pattern. Example: A neck is a home for a necklace, or a lake is a home for a raindrop. Draw pictures to go with your story.

1.

2.

Big Cats
Zoology

The beauty and power of big cats make them exciting to children. The tiger is the largest cat with facial markings as distinctive for each tiger as are fingerprints for humans. Lions have the loudest roar and live in families called prides. The cheetah is the fastest animal on land over short distances. Leopards have spotted coats and usually live alone or in a small group. Often confused with the leopard, a jaguar's coat has a dot inside a spot.

Children's Books

Bemelmans, L. (1939). *Madeline*. New York: The Viking Press.
  Children love Madeline who was not afraid of anything, even tigers.

Carle, E. (1987). *Have You Seen My Cat?* New York: Scholastic Inc.
  Repetitive text and Carle's characteristic illustrations lead the reader through a search for a pet cat, encountering all the big cats along the way.

De Regniers, B. (1964). *May I Bring a Friend?* New York: Atheneum.
  A boy brings his friends the lions to visit the king and queen.

Fatio, L. (1954). *The Happy Lion.* New York: McGraw-Hill Book Company, Inc.
  The first in a series of books about the happy lion in a French village.

Hoffman, M. (1985). *Lion*. Milwaukee: Raintree Children's Books.
  Packed with information about lions that is just right for early learners.

Hoffman, M. (1983). *Tiger*. Milwaukee: Raintree Children's Books.
  Beautiful photographs and primary-level text tell all about tigers.

Lester, J. (1989). *How Many Spots Does a Leopard Have?* New York: Scholastic Inc.
  Many animals try to count the leopard's spots with a surprising answer.

Divergent Topics

Consider activities with a circus or zoo theme if your class responds well to a study of cats. A comparison of wild animals and their domesticated counterparts offers another direction for exploration.

Scientific Observation

Arrange for a pet cat (and owner) to visit your class. While the children keep their distance, ask the owner to play with the cat. Children observe the cat; many of the movements (pouncing, striking, washing, clawing) are similar to those of the big cats. On a chart summarize the observations of the class.

Creeping and Pouncing

After observing a cat, provide plenty of space for children to become cats. Encourage the children to imitate the movements of the cat. "The Old Gray Cat" is fun to sing and play.

How Many Spots Does a Leopard Have?

Read the short tale *How Many Spots Does a Leopard Have?* to the class. Children then draw large leopards, putting lots of spots on their leopards. During the week ask children to show their drawings to the class. Classmates guess the number of spots on each leopard; then the class counts together. Write the correct number on each drawing and post on the bulletin board.

GA1465

To the Tiger in the Zoo . . .

After reading *Madeline*, ask children what they would say to the tiger in the zoo. Record the answers and have children draw illustrations for a class book. Then ask what the children might say to tigers in their yards! Compare the answers to the two questions.

Cat Snacks

For a tiger snack, provide graham crackers or slices of party rye bread and canned cheese that can be squeezed out in stripes. Set up this activity in a learning center. Children may eat their snacks immediately, or you may want them to save them on paper plates (with their names on them) for a group tiger feast.

A similar lion snack can be made with a round cracker. Spread the cracker with peanut butter and yellow cream cheese or other cheese spread. Add grated cheese or shredded coconut around the edges.

Zoo Bus

If you live near a zoo, plan a field trip to the cat section. Arrange for a zookeeper to talk with the class about big cats. Children will be able to ask questions about the cats and observe them closely.

The Painted Tiger

Set up the easel with orange and black paint. You are sure to get some wonderful tiger paintings to display in the room.

Stripes of a Different Color

After learning about tigers and other big cats, introduce the children to an artist who used stripes in interesting designs. Piet Mondrian (1872-1944) painted large canvases containing very straight black lines and blocks of color–often light blue, red, and yellow–on a white background. Examples of Mondrian's work will be found in art books at the public library.

Be sure that the children notice the use of right angles in Mondrian's paintings. There are no curves or swirls in these works. What a contrast to many of Van Gogh's paintings which are made up of curves and swirls!

Give each child a 9" x 12" (22.86 x 30.48 cm) sheet of white construction paper. Provide 1/2" (1.25 cm) and 1/4" (.6 cm) black strips of construction paper of different lengths. Also put out squares and rectangles of colored construction paper from 1/2" to 3" (1.25 to 7.62 cm) long. Demonstrate laying the strips and blocks out on the paper before gluing anything down. Tell the children it is like working a puzzle; you want to be sure you have every piece in just the right place. The last step is to glue the strips and blocks in place.

These collages make a striking bulletin board. The title might be "In the Style of Piet Mondrian (1872-1944)." Add a comment to the display to inform visitors that Mondrian worked with paint, but the class has simulated his work with paper.

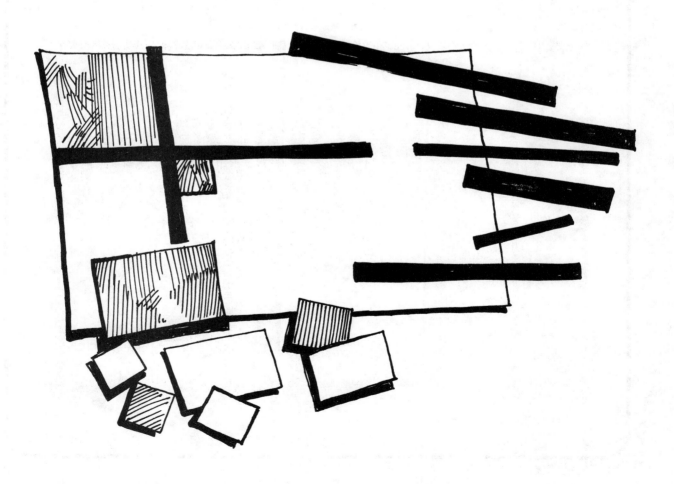

Endangered Cats

For a long time hunters killed the big cats to sell their fur. New laws now protect the cats. Big cats are still in danger because they need large areas to search for food. Many forests and grasslands are being destroyed by people. This means the big cats don't have many places to live. Another name for this problem is *loss of habitat.*

Draw your favorite big cat in the space below. Draw the cat's habitat. Write a sentence that will tell people to save the cat's home.

GA1465

Have You Seen My Cat?

The book by Eric Carle called *Have You Seen My Cat?* has pictures of many big cats. Draw your own pictures of the big cats in the spaces on this page.

Fastest Cat	**Spotted Cat**
This is a _____.	This is a _____.
Largest Cat	**Loudest Cat**
This is a _____.	This is a _____.

GA1465

Insects

Entomology

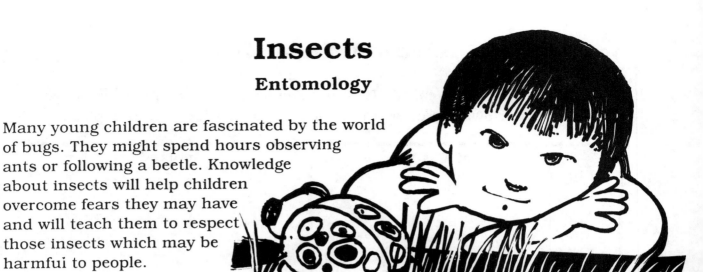

Many young children are fascinated by the world of bugs. They might spend hours observing ants or following a beetle. Knowledge about insects will help children overcome fears they may have and will teach them to respect those insects which may be harmful to people.

Background Information

All insects have distinct characteristics. To be an insect, the animal must have three body parts–a *head* for eyes, mouth, and antennae; a *thorax* (middle section) where wings are attached; an *abdomen* that contains the heart, digestive system, and breathing organs. Insects do not have bones, but they do have an *exoskeleton*. This exterior skeleton is a hard crust that protects the softer inner parts. The exoskeleton cannot grow, so the insect must shed the skeleton as it gets larger. Spiders and centipedes are not insects, but caterpillars are in the insect group.

Children's Books

Aardema, V. (1975). *Why Mosquitoes Buzz in People's Ears*. New York: Dial.

> This African folktale explains why the mosquito is so pesky.

Brinckloe, J. (1985). *Fireflies!* New York: Macmillan Publishing Company.

> Soft twilight illustrations capture the magic of catching fireflies and the good feeling of setting them free.

Caudill, R. (1964). *A Pocketful of Cricket*. New York: Holt, Rinehart and Winston.

> Jay collects pieces of the countryside as he brings in the cows, but his adopted cricket gets him into trouble at school.

Holley, B. (1986). *Bugs & Critters*. Milwaukee: Penworthy Publishing Company.

> Excellent fact-filled resource book for children.

Kirkpatrick, R. (1978). *Look at Insects*. Milwaukee: Raintree Children's Books.

> Primary reading level and bright pictures make this book a good one to have in the classroom.

Divergent Topics

Your class may be interested in spiders, flight, first aid, animals that live in communities, or metamorphosis.

Sing It! Know It

To help children learn the three body parts of insects, sing this song. Encourage children to add verses as they discover more facts about insects.

Tune: "Are You Sleeping?"

Head, thorax, abdomen,
Head, thorax, abdomen.
I have 3 body parts.
I have 3 body parts.
Add wings and my antennae,
Add wings and my antennae,
And six long legs,
And six long legs!

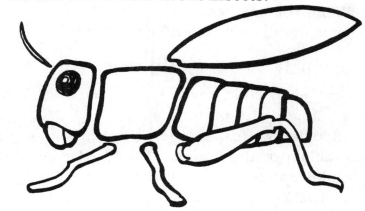

Insect Musicians

After reading *A Pocketful of Cricket* or *The Very Quiet Cricket*, have children write or dictate their feelings about crickets: "I like to hear crickets because _____" or "I don't like to hear crickets because _____ _____." Make a class graph of the number who like and don't like to hear crickets.

Insect Pests

Read *Why Mosquitoes Buzz in People's Ears*. Have children make stick puppets for the characters in the story and write a script for the puppet show. What other insect pests do the children know about?

Floppy Butterflies

Cut butterflies with large wings from wallpaper scraps. Fold the paper in the middle (where the butterfly's body would be) and tape it to a pipe cleaner or chenille stick. As children hold the sticks, they can make the wings appear to fly.

Hop, Crawl, Buzz-z-z-z

In an open area in the classroom or outdoors, children move like the insect you call out. Butterfly, grasshopper, ant, caterpillar, and firefly are easy to do. When you say bee or wasp, everyone shouts "Buzz-z-z-z!" Spice up this activity by listening to a recording of "The Flight of the Bumblebee."

Fireflies!

Give each child several paper jars, similar to the pattern at right. On each jar write a numeral, a math problem or draw a set of dots. The child "catches" the correct number of fireflies in each jar. If the jar has 4 dots, then the child adds 4 fireflies. For a jar that says, "3 + 5" the child adds 8 fireflies. To add interest, children can make fireflies by dipping the eraser end of a pencil in yellow paint, then touching the jar.

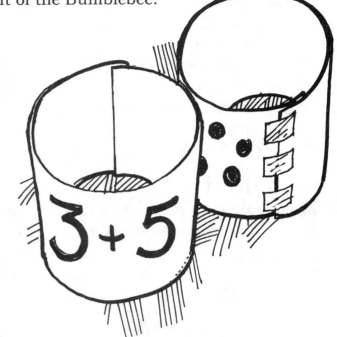

Feeding Time

Outdoors spread crumbs on the ground (away from the building). Wait a little while, then return to see if any insects have discovered the feast. Observe the ants and other insects as they move the crumbs.

Top of the Hill

Use the pattern on the next page to make an anthill from poster board. Glue the poster board hill to construction paper. Children lay manila paper over the anthill pattern and make a crayon rubbing. When the anthill is finished, add ants. The ants may be fingerprints, or they may be dabbed on with cotton swabs dipped in black paint.

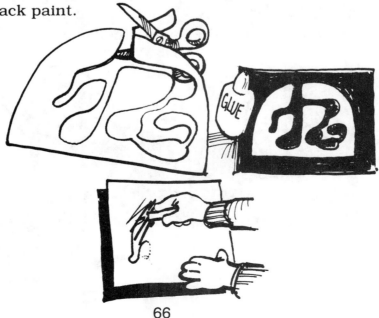

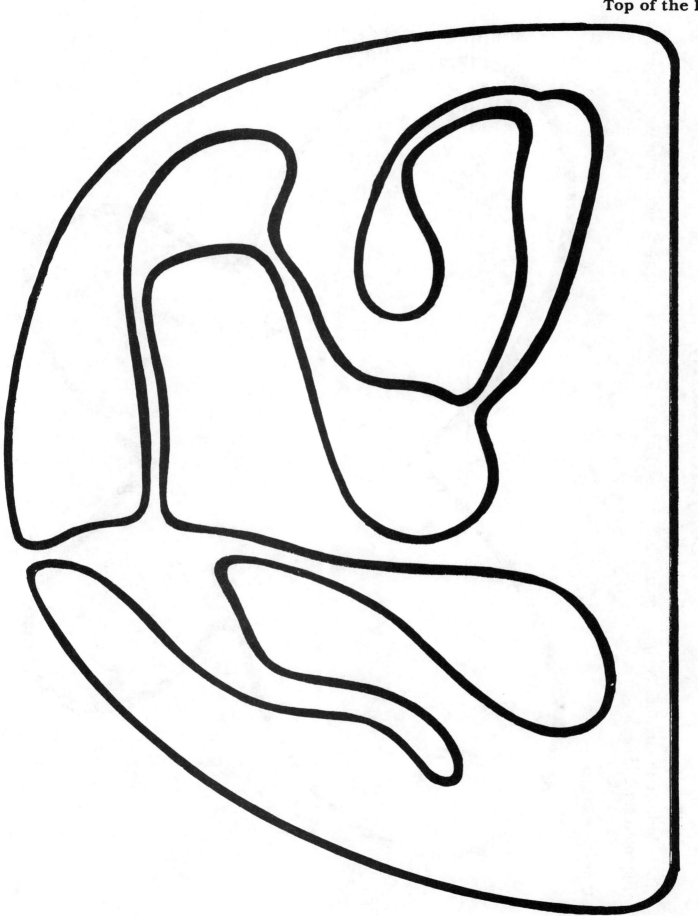

67

GA1465

Copycat Butterfly

The coloring on butterflies is *symmetrical*. That means the left side looks like the right side. Color your butterfly so that both sides look the same.

68

All About Insects

Draw three body parts of an insect.

How many legs does an insect have? _____
   Add these legs to your drawing.

What helps the insect fly? _____
   Add these to your drawing.

Most insects smell with these two things on their heads._____
   Add these to your insect drawing.

Insects have eyes on their _____.
   Give your insect some eyes.

Insects do not have _____.
   Insect skeletons are on the outside of the body.

A _____ is not an insect.

Trees

Botany/Forestry

The study of trees touches on botany, conservation and ecology, and aesthetics. Concepts in this unit will include the parts of a tree, the products of a tree, identifying trees, and the value of trees.

Children's Books

Althea. (1988). *Trees*. Longman Group U.S.A. Inc.
  One of the life cycle series written for young children.
Bulla, C. (1960). *A Tree Is a Plant*. Englewood Cliffs, NJ: Thomas Y. Crowell Company.
  Using an apple tree as an example, this book depicts the tree through four seasons.
Garelick, M., and Brenner, B. (1979). *The Tremendous Tree Book*. New York: Four Winds Press.
  Large, clear illustrations identify parts of the tree and uses.
Kirkpatrick, R. (1978). *Look at Trees*. Milwaukee: Raintree Children's Books.
  Helpful illustrations and simple text cover basic information on trees.
Lambert, D. (1990). *Forests*. Mahwah, NJ: Troll Associates.
  Good information and pictures on this topic.
Udry, J. (1956). *A Tree Is Nice*. New York: Harper & Row Publishers.
  The classic Caldecott award winner detailing the wonders of trees.

People to Know

As your class explores trees, you will probably discuss Johnny Appleseed, who planted trees across the country. The children will also enjoy learning about Sacajawea, the Native American woman who served as a guide for the Lewis and Clark expedition; and about John Muir of California, an early environmentalist.

Divergent Topics

Your class unit on trees might serve as a springboard to study some of these topics: conservation, recycling, air pollution, furniture design and construction, papermaking and publishing.

GA1465

A Tree Collection

The entire class can participate in this project for several weeks. Children bring leaves to class, pieces of bark, seeds and seed pods from trees. The goal is to have many different types of trees represented. As the items arrive, have a committee identify and label each one; several good resource books will be needed for this task. Another committee will need to arrange plenty of space to display the collection. One group of children will determine the layout of the exhibit. There will be many other jobs to do as the project progresses. The children will not only learn about trees, but they will also practice classification and language skills and group decision making.

Take a Closer Look

Provide magnifiers, newsprint, and "unwrapped" crayons for the children. After examining an item from the tree collection, children make crayon rubbings of the leaves, bark, and seeds. Some of the rubbings might be cut out and mounted on cards to be used for matching games. Younger students will find the leaves easiest to work with. More experienced artists will enjoy the challenge of working with bark or pinecones. Using the magnifier and looking for detail in the rubbings will encourage children to examine the tree collection more closely.

GA1465

Evaluating Trees

Read *A Tree Is Nice*. Each child writes or dictates a statement about a tree: "A tree is nice because _____." A drawing of a tree on the page will complete the activity. If the pages are bound together, this activity produces a nice class book for the library corner.

Up the Wall

Enlist the help of the class to create a huge tree on one wall of the classroom. You might use butcher paper or large pieces of newsprint, painting the trunk brown and adding construction paper leaves.

As children learn about plants and animals that depend on trees for their existence, they draw pictures of the species and tape them to the class tree. Older children or an adult will make large word cards to label the drawings. Encourage children to copy the names of the tree-dependent animals in a blank book or notebook. Have them draw pictures of the animals to go with the words.

Get by the Tree

The song "Tree Fell Down," from the Hap Palmer record *Easy Does It*, is a refreshing break from classroom routine. The tree falls down on a windy day and the children must move over and under the tree, then find their own way to get by the tree. A broom handle or meterstick can be used for the tree.

What's Missing?

Use items from the class tree collection to play this game. An easy game might use a nut, a leaf, and a piece of bark. Children close their eyes; the leader removes one object. Children guess what's missing. Increase the difficulty by using items that are similar.

This Is Nuts

Collect assorted nuts (buy some to fill in the collection). Place the nuts in a basket for sorting, counting, and matching. A shape lotto board can be made for children to match nuts.

In another area of the room, add a pan of nuts and a nutcracker. Include a container for shells. Children crack and eat nuts. This is a good time for developing conversation, and the use of the nutcracker strengthens small muscles.

Save all those nutshells for a really nutty art day! Glue small pieces of shell on paper for collages. Glue pieces together to make nut sculptures.

GA1465

Walk and Roll!

In the fall bring in a box of leaves. Empty the leaves in a corner of the room, and invite the children to walk and roll in the pile. Define the leaf play area with masking tape on the floor or by using a large shallow box to hold the leaves. Encourage the children to listen, touch, and look at the leaves. Because this activity will be so popular, the leaves will probably need to be freshened or replaced several times during the week.

The Art of the Trees

Attractive leaf prints can be made with acrylic paint that captures the brilliance of autumn color. Cover a table with newspaper. Pour small amounts of paint into dishes. Paint the underside of the leaf with one color of paint; then press the leaf onto paper or fabric. Show the children how to use a small amount of paint so that the intricate veins can be seen in the print. For variations of this activity, use a stamp pad or a sponge coated with paint; press the leaf onto the pad or sponge and then print.

Bough painting requires plenty of space because the children may sling paint as they get into this activity! Dip small boughs of evergreen in green paint and press or brush on paper. Tell the class they already know how to paint with brushes, so today they will paint with trees. Allow the children to experiment with the boughs and develop their own techniques. Your room will smell great, thanks to the freshly cut boughs!

In the Park

Show the class a print of the painting by Georges Seurat, *Sunday Afternoon on the Island of La Grande Jatte*. Allow plenty of time for the children to notice all the detail in the painting. Tell the children that the original painting is very large; it covers a whole wall in a museum!

Show several other examples of the work of Seurat. Children will probably comment that his paintings look like lots of dots. Seurat used the point of his brush to build combinations of dots that created pictures. The technique that he invented is called *pointillism*.

Seurat often painted outdoor scenes, and the children will find trees in many of his paintings. The public library and school encyclopedias should provide several examples of Seurat's painting.

The children can create pictures in the style of Georges Seurat using crayons, paper, and sandpaper. Tape a $4^1/_2$" x 6" (11.41 x 15.24 cm) piece of sandpaper to the top of a table or desk. Place a $4^1/_2$" x 6" (11.41 x 15.24 cm) piece of drawing paper over the sandpaper. As the child draws with crayon, points of color will appear on the paper which will resemble the work of Seurat. Remind the children to fill in all the space on the paper. Mount the finished drawings on 9" x 12" (22.86 x 30.48 cm) pieces of construction paper. Label the pictures "In the Style of Georges Seurat (1859-1891)."

A Tree in All Seasons

Think about how a tree looks in spring, in summer, in fall, and in winter. In the four boxes on this page, draw a picture of a tree in each season.

Spring	**Summer**
Fall	**Winter**

GA1465

Our Tree Collection

We collected _____ leaves. These leaves were from _____ different trees. Draw some leaves here.

We collected _____ pieces of bark.
Draw some pieces of bark here.

We collected _____ seeds. These seeds came from _____ different trees.

We collected _____ seed pods.
Draw some seed pods here.

We collected things from these trees:

_____

_____

_____

_____

_____

GA1465

Flowers

Botany/Horticulture

Although spring is often the time when flowers are noticed, your class will find a study of flowers interesting at any time of the year. Students will learn about wildflowers and cultivated flowers, the structure of a flower, and the importance of flowers to us.

Children's Books

Althea. (1988). *Flowers.* Longman Group U.S.A. Inc.
   One of a series of life cycle books with excellent pictures.
Carlstrom, N. (1987). *Wild, Wild Sunflower Child Anna.* New York: Scholastic Inc.
   Anna runs wild through meadows and forests, discovering plant life. Bright, summery illustrations.
De Paola, T. (1988). *The Legend of the Indian Paintbrush.* New York: Scholastic Inc.
   Retelling of the legend of the Indian paintbrush wildflower with breathtaking illustrations.
Kirkpatrick, R. (1978). *Look at Flowers.* Milwaukee: Raintree Children's Books.
   Clear illustrations and simple, informative text.
Krauss, R. (1949). *The Happy Day.* New York: Harper & Row Publishers.
   Very easy reading. The forest animals rush through the snow to find something very exciting.
Laird, E. (1990). *Rosy's Garden: A Child's Keepsake of Flowers.* New York: Philomel Books.
   Filled with information about flowers–how flowers got their names, well-known flower poetry, flower games and crafts, and more! The illustrations are beautiful, soft pastel watercolors.

People to Know

Lady Bird Johnson has worked for many years to encourage the propagation of wildflowers. She has written a guide to wildflowers that contains lovely illustrations.

Vincent Van Gogh painted a number of still life subjects that included flowers. The public library will have examples of his work to show the class.

Divergent Topics

If your class enjoys the unit on flowers, they may want to explore smells in more detail or learn about edible plants.

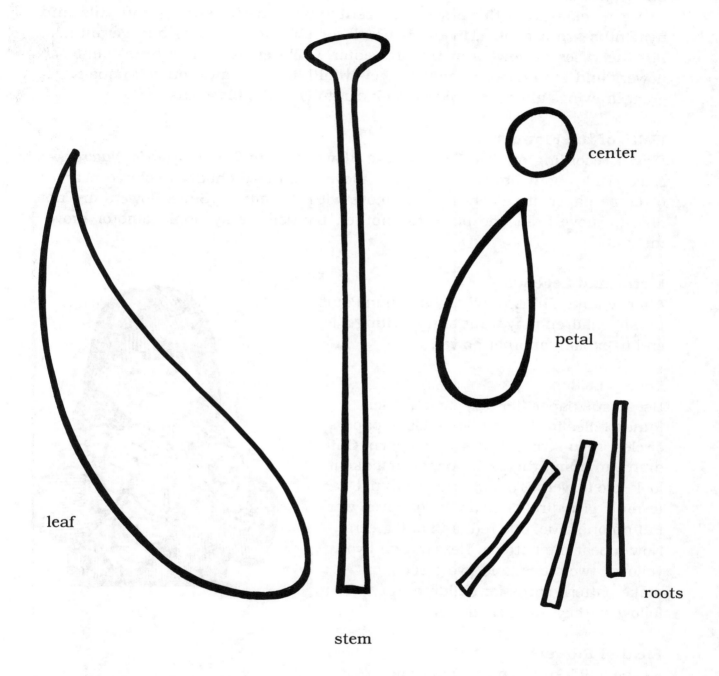

center

petal

leaf

roots

stem

Getting It All Together

Use the patterns on this page to make felt plant pieces for the flannel board. Leave the pieces in the library corner for a few days; then play games such as I Spy or What's Missing with a small group. Use the felt pieces as objects for the games.

See It; Draw It

Bring to class real flowers of different types. In the spring daffodils and hyacinths are available; in the fall look for chrysanthemums and geraniums. Put the vases of flowers in the art center. Children take time to examine the flowers and then choose one that they would like to draw. You will usually get great drawings after the children look carefully at the blossoms.

Waltz of the Flowers

Play a recording of "The Waltz of the Flowers" from Tchaikovsky's *Nutcracker Suite*. Talk about how flowers might move; then give children colored scarves or crepe paper streamers as they move with the music. Since flowers are not able to move from one place to another, try using only nonlocomotor movements.

Myths and Legends

After reading *The Legend of the Indian Paint-brush*, children may want to try writing a legend to explain another flower.

Lovely Leis

Use tissue paper "flowers" to make leis. Punch holes in the middle of tissue paper circles; then string the tissue on yarn. Children can crimp the tissue paper to make it look like flowers. To add practice in patterning, give directions as the children work. Put on one blue, one red, and one green. Now repeat the pattern. Next put on two yellows, two blues, and two greens, or make pattern cards for children to follow as they make their leis.

Field of Flowers

As the children learn the names of both wild and cultivated flowers, begin a class mural. Provide the paper and paint or markers, but allow the class to decide how the mural will look and what flowers will be included. The children can add to this project throughout the unit.

Sunflowers and Irises

Show the class several reproductions of Van Gogh's paintings. Look for those that include flowers. Point out the interesting "bumpy" look to many of his paintings. Van Gogh used curves and swirls of paint in his pictures. Many of Van Gogh's works use a lot of yellow–perhaps a good companion to the book *Wild, Wild Sunflower Child Anna* when you celebrate Yellow Day.

The children create their own masterpieces in the style of Van Gogh by applying thick tempera paint to paper or poster board with craft sticks. Mount the finished paintings on construction paper or contrasting poster board. Label each with the information "In the Style of Vincent Van Gogh (1853-1890)."

Many Flowers, Many Ways

Make sorting cards from seed catalog illustrations or from brochures obtained from florist shops. Each card should show one type of flower. Working with a small group of children, ask them to sort the flowers. Do not offer cues to sorting unless the children seem to be stumped. Then tell them to sort the cards in a different way. Continue sorting in various ways for several rounds. Children may sort by color, size, or types of petals, for example.

GA1465

Flower Hike

Flowers are pretty in yards and in fields. It is good to let flowers grow and not pick them. Take a walk to look for flowers. Draw the flowers you see. Write the name of each flower if you know it.

Name of flower _____
    Draw the flower here.

Name of flower _____
    Draw the flower here.

Name of flower _____
    Draw the flower here.

GA1465

Family Fun Sheet
Our Visit to a Flower Place

Dear Family:

Visit a "flower place" with your child. This might be a florist shop, a landscape nursery, a botanical garden, or your own backyard. Help your child fill out the report sheet below and return it to school to share with us. Have fun!

We visited _____

Some of the flowers we saw were _____

_____

The flowers needed this kind of special care:_____

_____

This is how the people here learned about flowers:_____

_____

I think this was a good place to visit to see flowers because _____

_____

Draw a picture of some of the flowers you saw.

Sharing the World of Art

"I don't know anything about art." Many preschool and elementary teachers make this claim. If we believe that education is a lifelong experience, however, then the teacher will enjoy learning along with the students. Extensive training in art is not necessary, just as an in-depth knowledge of science or mathematics is not required to teach these subjects to young children. The art activities throughout this book will get you started on discovering art with your class.

Benefits of Art in the Classroom

As children examine works of art by different artists from different periods in history and from different cultures, a tolerance for differences is fostered. Children see that there is more than one way to paint a flower, that being different does not mean being wrong or funny.

Experiences with art help build children's confidence in their own ideas and problem-solving abilities. As children work to express their ideas with paint or paper and glue, they develop competence in managing frustration and disappointment. They learn to evaluate their own work.

Appreciation for high-quality art must be cultivated. If children see only cartoon characters, they may not have a taste for the works of the masters. For example, a spring bulletin board might use a reproduction of Van Gogh's *Sunflowers* rather than Minnie Mouse holding a bouquet.

Sources for Art Reproductions

The most readily available and cheapest source for artworks is a calendar. For about $10.00 you will get twelve to fourteen reproductions that are perfect for use in the classroom.

Museum shops offer postcard reprints of their collections. These are great for the children to use in playing games. The children might sort the postcards according to dominant color or by subject matter.

If you buy duplicates of each postcard, children can play memory games with them.

Many school systems have sets of art reproductions. These may be at a secondary art department or library. Art teachers and librarians are usually happy to share their materials with the younger grades.

The public library is a valuable source for examples of art. All of the artists and works mentioned in this book should be easily found at your local library. If you have access to a university library, you will find a wealth of material. One note of caution in using art books from the library (or any other source): many artists have explored the human figure in their work. Families may not feel comfortable with their children viewing nudes, even if they are masterpieces. Know your families and play it safe. This means that you may not be able to put out some art books for children to browse through; you may need to show the appropriate works, then put away the book. This is unfortunate, but it is a fact of reality when we are working with other people's children. Be very careful not to intrude on any family's values.

Field Trips

If you live near a museum or gallery, take the class to visit. Several short trips during the year are of more value than one marathon in which you see the entire museum. Even if you can take only one trip, plan it carefully so that the children do not tire or become bored. Work with the museum staff to plan a trip that matches the interests of the class and supports the art and science concepts you have learned.

Another good field trip is a visit to the high school art department. The children will be able to see and touch the tools and equipment used by artists. If the department includes a ceramic or sculpture area, the class can see that art is more than painting.

At the high school or at a gallery, your class will be interested in watching an artist at work. The group may be able to interview the artist.

Some of the questions that might be asked are

    How did you learn to be an artist?

    How do you know what to paint?

    How long does it take to paint a picture?

    What is your favorite color?

    Do you have a dog?

       (Children should be able to ask anything!)

    Do you sell your paintings?

GA1465

In the Style of . . .

After children have some time to examine the works of an artist, they need a hands-on experience. Provide appropriate materials with which the children can create their own work "In the Style of . . . ." Be sure to write this on the child's product: "In the Style of Vincent Van Gogh (1853-1890)." This is the easiest way to communicate with parents about your art activities in the classroom.

Sometimes children will simulate an artist's work with materials other than those used by the artist. For example, Piet Mondrian was a painter, but children will use construction paper and glue to create pictures in the style of Mondrian. Be sure the children understand that Mondrian used paint, but we are going to use paper.

Language Experiences

Art reproductions can be used very successfully for language experience activities. On Blue Day, for example, offer a choice of three to four artworks that have blue as the predominant color. Then ask children to tell stories about the pictures. Picasso's *Three Musicians* lends itself to telling stories about what instruments they would like to play. Some works can be used for a "you are there" approach; children pretend they are in the picture and tell what is happening.

Concrete Reproduction

Still life and abstract paintings, in particular, can be used for this activity. Cézanne has painted still lifes that include bowls of fruit. Set out a bowl, the fruit and the reproduction; then encourage children to make the real objects look like the painting. Mondrian's designs can be easily reproduced on the flannel board with strips and blocks of felt.

GA1465

Artists for Children

The artists listed below are of interest to children and can easily be copied by the students. Many of these artists have been included in the units in this book. Those that have not been included are accompanied by suggestions for how to study them.

Vincent Van Gogh (1853-1890): See "Flowers" and "The Moon and the Stars."

Claude Monet (1840-1926): See "Light."

Jackson Pollock (1912-1956): See "Wind."

Wassily Kandinsky (1866-1944): See "Chemistry."

Georges Seurat (1859-1891): See "Trees."

Piet Mondrian (1872-1944): See "Big Cats."

Alexander Calder (1898-1976): See "Gravity, Balance and Inertia."

Georges Rouault (1871-1958): The child paints the outlines with black tempera. When this is completely dry, fill in the outline with jewel-toned tempera.

Paul Klee (1879-1940): Prepare crayon scratch boards. The child scratches a design with paper clips, forks, etc.

Pierre Auguste Renoir (1841-1919): Use tempera with small brushes. Encourage the use of red in each picture.

Frederic Remington (1861-1909): Simulate bronzes by building papier-mâché animals. Spray with metallic gold paint. Paint over gold with a black tempera wash.

Hans Holbein the Younger (1497-1543): Children paint portraits of their best friends. Point out how the artist paints in the background and often paints only the shoulders and head.

Displaying Students' Art

Display the children's best efforts in the classroom or hallway. Mount each painting or drawing on poster board or construction paper so that a border results. The best size paper is often 4¹/₂" x 6" (11.41 x 15.24 cm) for the child's art, with a 9" x 12" (22.86 x 30.48 cm) paper under it for display.

Larger works can be matted with poster board or construction paper, taping the paper to the mat. The mat or the border of the mounted work provides a good place to write the child's name and the artist being simulated.

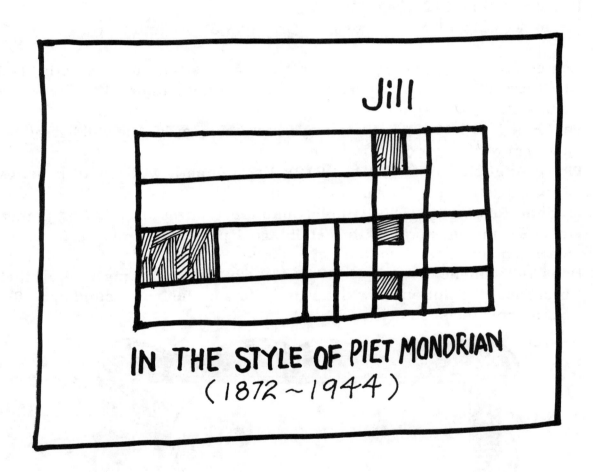

GA1465

Bibliography

Aardema, V. (1981). *Bringing the Rain to Kapiti Plain*. New York: Dial Books for Young Readers, E.P. Dutton, Inc.

Aardema, V. (1975). *Why Mosquitoes Buzz in People's Ears*. New York: Dial.

Althea. (1988). *Flowers*. Longman Group U.S.A. Inc.

Althea. (1988). *Trees*. Longman Group U.S.A. Inc.

Asch, F. (1985). *Bear Shadow*. New York: Scholastic Inc.

Barton, B. (1981). *Building a House*. New York: Greenwillow Books.

Bemelmans, L. (1939). *Madeline*. New York: The Viking Press.

Bemelmans, L. (1953). *Madeline's Rescue*. New York: The Viking Press.

Brinckloe, J. (1985). *Fireflies!* New York: Macmillan Publishing Company.

Brown, M. (1982). *Shadow*. New York: Macmillan Publishing Company.

Brown, M. (1947). *Stone Soup*. New York: Charles Scribner's Sons.

Bulla, C. (1960). *A Tree Is a Plant*. Englewood Cliffs, NJ: Thomas Y. Crowell Company.

Bulla, C. (1962). *What Makes a Shadow?* Englewood Cliffs, NJ: Thomas Y. Crowell Company.

Carle, E. (1987). *Have You Seen My Cat?* New York: Scholastic Inc.

Carle, E. (1977). *Papa, Please Get the Moon for Me*. New York: Scholastic Inc.

Carlstrom, N. (1987). *Wild, Wild Sunflower Child Anna*. New York: Scholastic Inc.

Caudill, R. (1964). *A Pocketful of Cricket*. New York: Holt, Rinehart and Winston.

Charlip, R. (1966). *Mother, Mother, I Feel Sick; Send for the Doctor Quick, Quick, Quick!* New York: Parents' Magazine Press.

Cohlene, T. (1990). *Ka-ha-si and the Loon: An Eskimo Legend*. Vero Beach, FL: The Rourke Corporation, Inc.

Cohlene, T. (1990). *Quillworker: A Cheyenne Legend*. Vero Beach, FL: The Rourke Corporation, Inc.

Day, A. (1990). *River Parade*. New York: Scholastic Inc.

De Paola, T. (1988). *The Legend of the Indian Paintbrush*. New York: Scholastic Inc.

De Regniers, B. (1964). *May I Bring a Friend?* New York: Atheneum.

Fatio, L. (1954). *The Happy Lion*. New York: McGraw-Hill Book Company, Inc.

Fowler, A. (1991). *The Sun Is Always Shining Somewhere*. Chicago: Children's Press.

Gans, R. (1964). *Icebergs*. Englewood Cliffs, NJ: Thomas Y. Crowell Company.

Garelick, M., and Brenner, B. (1979). *The Tremendous Tree Book*. New York: Four Winds Press.

Goor, R., and Goor, N. (1981). *Shadows: Here, There, and Everywhere*. New York: McGraw-Hill Book Company.

Greenfield, E. (1976). *First Pink Light*. New York: Thomas Y. Crowell Company.

Hatch, S. (1973). *Wind Is to Feel*. New York: Coward, McCann and Geoghegan, Inc.

Hoberman, M. (1978). *A House Is a House for Me*. New York: The Viking Press.

Hoffman, M. (1985). *Lion*. Milwaukee: Raintree Children's Books.

Hoffman, M. (1983). *Tiger*. Milwaukee: Raintree Children's Books.

Holley, B. (1986). *Bugs & Critters*. Milwaukee: Penworthy Publishing Company.

Hutchins, P. (1974). *The Wind Blew*. New York: Macmillan Publishing Company.

GA1465

Jennings, T. (1982). *Light and Color*. Chicago: Children's Press.

Jennings, T. (1982). *Rocks and Soil*. Chicago: Children's Press.

Kirkpatrick, R. (1978). *Look at Flowers*. Milwaukee: Raintree Children's Books.

Kirkpatrick, R. (1978). *Look at Insects*. Milwaukee: Raintree Children's Books.

Kirkpatrick, R. (1978). *Look at Trees*. Milwaukee: Raintree Children's Books.

Krauss, R. (1949). *The Happy Day*. New York: Harper & Row Publishers.

Laird, E. (1990). *Rosy's Garden: A Child's Keepsake of Flowers*. New York: Philomel Books.

Lambert, D. (1990). *Forests*. Mahwah, NJ: Troll Associates.

Lefkowitz, R. (1972). *Matter All Around You*. New York: Parents' Magazine Press.

Lefkowitz, R. (1975). *Push! Pull! Stop! Go! A Book About Forces and Motions*. New York: Parents' Magazine Press.

Lester, J. (1989). *How Many Spots Does a Leopard Have?* New York: Scholastic Inc.

Lexau, J. (1964). *Benjie*. New York: The Dial Press.

Lillegard, D., and Stoker, W. (1987). *I Can Be a Plumber*. Chicago: Children's Press.

Lovik, C. (1987). *Andy and the Tire*. New York: Scholastic Inc.

Macaulay, D. (1978). *Castle*. New York: Houghton.

Martin, C. (1978). *I Can Be a Weather Forecaster*. Chicago: Children's Press.

McCloskey, R. (1957). *Time of Wonder*. New York: The Viking Press.

McKissack, P. (1988). *Mirandy and Brother Wind*. New York: Alfred A. Knopf.

Nodset, J. (1963). *Who Took the Farmer's Hat?* New York: Scholastic Inc.

Orii, E., and Orii, M. (1989). *Simple Science Experiments with Light*. Milwaukee: Gareth Stevens Children's Books.

Parramon, J., and Vendrell, C., (1984). *The Four Elements: Water*. New York: Barron's Education Services, Children's Press Choice.

Schwartz, J. (1965). *Uphill and Downhill*. New York: McGraw-Hill Book Company.

Simon, S. (1970). *Let's-Try-It-Out: Light and Dark*. New York: McGraw-Hill Book Company.

Sipiera, P. (1986). *I Can Be a Geologist*. Chicago: Children's Press.

Slobodkina, E. (1947). *Caps for Sale*. New York: Harper.

Spier, P. (1982). *Rain*. Garden City, NY: Doubleday Company, Inc.

Steig, W. (1969). *Sylvester and the Magic Pebble*. New York: Windmill Books.

Tobias, T. (1977). *Liquid or Solid? That's a Good Question!* Chicago: Children's Press.

Udry, J. (1956). *A Tree Is Nice*. New York: Harper & Row Publishers.

Wade, H. (1977). *Water*. Milwaukee: Raintree Publishers, Limited.

Wandelmaier, R. (1985). *Now I Know: Stars*. Mahwah, NJ: Troll Associates.

Wood, J. (1991). *Caves: An Underground Wonderland*. Milwaukee: Gareth Stevens Children's Books.

Yashima, T. (1958). *Umbrella*. New York: The Viking Press.

Yolen, J. (1987). *Owl Moon*. New York: Philomel Books.